——— ✦⋯✤⋯✦ ———

BECOMING COMPATIBLE

How to succeed in any relationship by understanding the key motivations of yourself and others.

MARK GUNGOR

Becoming Compatible By Mark Gungor
Book design by Debbie Bishop
Illustrations by Alfredo Montañe Vargas
Special thanks to Diane Brierley for contributing
her time and effort in the writing of this book.

For information, address inquiries to: info@laughyourway.com

www.markgungor.com

Printed in China

BECOMING
COMPATIBLE

**How to succeed in any relationship by understanding
the key motivations of yourself and others.**

MARK
GUNGOR

In loving memory of Terry J. Kohler

BECOMING
COMPATIBLE

**How to succeed in any relationship by understanding
the key motivations of yourself and others.**

MARK
GUNGOR

CONTENTS

CHAPTER ONE

BECOMING COMPATIBLE

CHAPTER ONE

BECOMING COMPATIBLE

I t is not unusual to meet with a couple in crisis that is struggling with the frustrations of two souls acting as one, and hear the complaint, "We are just not compatible." They feel they have made a big mistake in choosing to marry each other, because after the vows have been exchanged they eventually discover that they don't always think the same way or feel the same things. They unearth the reality that they may not share all the same interests and that they may even embrace different goals. And since they believe such a state is a sign of incompatibility, they assume the only answer is to end the marriage. After all, if two people are not compatible then there is no hope for marital success, right?

Actually...wrong.

The word for two people who always think and feel the same, share all the same interests and always embrace the same goals is not compatible, it's delusional. Two people will never invariably think and feel the same, share all the same interests or always embrace the same goals. That is absurd. Besides, that isn't even what the word compatible really means.

The word compatible comes from the Latin word *compati*, which literally means "to suffer with". A couple who can suffer with each other is, in fact, the very definition of compatible. Being compatible is not about reaching a state of nirvana, it is about having someone you can do life with. Life in all its ugly, messy, painful, glorious, wonderful and marvelous state.

And if you think about it, couples whose marriages fail often do so because they reach a point where they can no longer "suffer" with each other. The word we use to describe such a state is insufferable. When people reach the point where their marriage is insufferable, it is a bad place to be. It's like being water boarded...the very simple act of breathing seems impossible, causing the person being interrogated to willingly do or say anything just so they can breathe.

The saddest part of all of this is that people truly believe that having a compatible marriage vs an incompatible marriage (or an insufferable one) is pretty much a matter of chance. We're told, "If you are lucky, you will find someone you are compatible with. If you are unlucky, you will discover you are in an insufferable relationship where the only path to relief is divorce." We are fed nonsensical concepts like "the one," "soul mates" or "God's choice." But what if there are really no "soul mates" or what if there isn't that one "divinely ordained person" out there?

Think about it: If there is truly only ONE person just for you, what are your chances of finding that person among a population of billions? And as for the "divinely ordained person" ...let's think about that one for a moment.

Let us assume that God has truly chosen ONE person for everyone on Earth. Well, all it would take is for ONE person to get it wrong and the whole thing collapses!! If Alan is supposed to marry Juliet, but marries Susan instead...what is Juliet supposed to do? Now she marries Bill who was supposed to marry Sarah...what is Sarah supposed to do? Now Sarah marries Fred who was supposed to marry Wilma... (Now you have no Flintstones.)

What if the key to true compatibility is not a matter of chance – a one in a billion shot – or even divine ordination requiring great spiritual intuition?

What if people become compatible? What if they become compatible on purpose?

According to all surveys that have looked at successful people in life – in business, in talent and even in love – one thing becomes clear very quickly: They all got that way on purpose.

Oh, a business person seemingly stumbled across a great opportunity, but a close look always reveals that he or she worked very hard to find and ultimately take advantage of that opportunity. A musician may start out with a certain degree of natural talent, but every artist becomes great because they worked really hard at it – some practicing up to eight hours a day, every single day, for years, even decades.

And when interviewing couples that have been successfully married for 50, 60, 75 years and more, one thing always stands out: They worked very hard to get to where they are. In fact, many of those 75 year marriages started out as insufferable before they became compatible.

Bottom line – people become compatible intentionally.

Of course, the obvious question then becomes: How?

THE KEY

The key to succeeding with anyone – business partners, friends, family, children and especially a spouse is: Understanding. When you understand why people do what they do, it changes everything, even if it doesn't change anything.

For example:

You go to work tomorrow and Maryanne in the front office is being short tempered, emotional and/or impatient with everyone. Chances are your first instinct will be to pull her aside and read her the riot act, explaining that this is not acceptable behavior in a professional setting. But just before you pull her aside someone says to you, "Did you hear about poor Maryanne? Her mom died unexpectedly last night..."

Oh.

What happens? Everything changes – even though nothing changes at all. I mean, Maryanne may still be a mess, but now you know why she is acting that way. Now you are not angry with her, in fact, you begin to feel empathy for her.

Here is an actual story...

Some years ago Roger and Julie came to see me. Julie was in tears and Roger was at his wits' end. He would ask Julie to do some of the simplest things, only to see her melt in tears, anger and resentment. He told me that when Julie would come in the house she would just kick off her shoes and flop her jacket randomly on whatever chair or surface was closest. Roger would ask her to put her shoes orderly next to the door and hang her jacket in the closet near the door. Julie, however, would just come unglued.

During our session, I began to ask Julie why she was reacting the way she was. She finally opened up about how she was raised. She told of how her mother did not want to know she was there. She literally was forced to play in her closet, lest mom would see or hear her. And if there was one thing mom would not tolerate, it was that Julie's shoes were not put away or her jacket not hung properly. Her mother would shout at her, "I don't want to know you are even here!!"

I looked at her husband as she told her story, his eyes telling me he had never heard any of this before.

"Roger, did you ever know this about Julie's childhood?"

"No," he replied sheepishly.

I said, "Can you love her enough to allow her to leave a big enough mess so that you know she is home?"

"Yeah…I can do that."

You see, when you don't know why people do what they do, it will most likely just make you angry. When you know why, it tends to change things. Oh, you still may not like it, but you can suffer through it. You can become…compatible.

VIVE LA DIFFÉRENCE

I know you know this, but it is important to remind you: You and your spouse are different. In fact, it is these differences that caused you to be drawn to each other in the first place. But it doesn't take long before the very differences you found fascinating begin to annoy you.

And let's face it, every single argument in a relationship boils down to one very simple argument: Why can't you be more…like me? Well, the answer is very simple: Because they are not you. They have different experiences, different thought patterns, different motivations, different temperaments, different ways of responding to things, different… well, different everything.

As I just stated, the key to this is understanding. But here is the problem: We have been fed a line of bull from Hollywood that basically says that if people truly love you, they would know you. This is utter nonsense and pabulum. The truth is, people can love you dearly and have absolutely no idea why you do what you do or why you react the way you react.

And here is the real truth: If you don't tell them, they won't know.

Think this gets any easier? Nope. We just keep digging a deeper hole because the hard truth is this: The reason most people don't tell others why they act and respond the way they do, is because they DON'T KNOW WHY they act and respond the way they do!! In other words, they can't explain what they themselves don't even know. And if you don't understand you, how do you expect others to? Just because they say they love you?? Not a very reasonable or realistic expectation.

Who Am I??

This is the basic question every human being struggles to answer. The answer is important because if we don't understand who we are, we can never help others understand who we are. And if they don't understand us, they can't give us what we need.

The answer, however, is difficult because we didn't come with an instruction manual at birth telling us about ourselves or describing how we were wired. Even the simplest over-the-counter remedy comes with a label that describes what it is, what it should be used for and exactly how it should be used. But when we humans come into the world, we show up naked and totally helpless. Ideally, each new child would be surrounded by the hopes, dreams and open honesty of parents, grandparents, uncles, aunts, cousins and siblings – i.e. a healthy family. I believe this close family net was designed by God to act as a mirror for us so that in the loving and supportive faces of our family, we are able to catch glimpses of who we really are, what we truly look like and what we are capable of.

For thousands and thousands of years, human beings were surrounded by such an honest mirror. People would live their entire lives and die no more than a few miles from where they were born. Just looking out their front door they would be greeted by this network of involved family. Remember, there was no such thing as birth control. People had l-a-r-g-e families. In other words, if you went out the door you were likely to be inundated with grandparents, uncles and aunts and a small army of cousins. Through the feedback and honest reflection of a caring family, people could get a true sense of just who they were.

Sadly, since the industrial revolution, the Western world has witnessed the disintegration of this supportive family net. Today, family members are scattered all over the country. For most of us, the only glimpse we get of close family is during the holidays, as we rush in a seeming panic to spend just a few hours with this family member and that one. Yet, even in those brief gatherings of siblings and parental units, we are able to catch quick glimpses of the "mirror," reflections of ourselves from people who know us better than anyone.

Truth be told, though, most of us hate the brutal honesty we are faced with in our families. It causes us to think, "Thank God we don't live near them the rest of the year," but we fail to realize that this uncomfortable network of family is our best shot at getting an honest picture of who we really are. This assumes, of course, that we are part of a healthy family; and sadly, that is becoming more and more rare.

So many of today's families are made up of emotionally broken and dysfunctional people that it is unlikely they could provide much of a healthy mirror for anyone close to them anyway. And even sadder is the number of people who come out of this family dysfunction with skewed, flawed and broken perceptions of themselves.

Many are the men and women who believe they are stupid, worthless, no good. Far too often they have incorrectly learned that they are a nothing, a nobody who will never amount to anything. Stripped of their self-confidence, self-worth, and self-esteem, they struggle through childhood and adolescence, then go stumbling into adulthood with no idea why they feel, act and react the way they do.

So where does that leave us? With millions of people who are unsure of themselves and not really knowing who they are.

People can become compatible intentionally through understanding what motivates the other person. However, most people cannot clearly explain to another what truly motivates them. When this happens, there is a good chance that instead of becoming sufferable (compatible), many people's relationships will become insufferable (incompatible). And when relationships become insufferable the most natural reaction will be to walk away from that relationship.

(And by the way, these truths hold for every relationship, not just marital. Your interaction with friends, family, in-laws, church members, children, step-children, work and, yes, even your spouse will become insufferable if you don't know what motivates them and they don't know what motivates you.)

Which brings us to the reason for this book. In these pages, I am going to help you to better understand you, show you how you can more clearly explain yourself to the people around you and, if you apply these tools to the people in your life, to help you better understand them.

CHAPTER TWO

THE FLAG PAGE

CHAPTER TWO

THE
FLAG PAGE

I n order to walk you through this journey of self-discovery, we are going to use a special on-line tool designed to help give you great insight into just who you are and how you can more effectively communicate yourself to others. I am going to need you to go to a computer and take a very simple test. It's called The Flag Page. (I'll explain the peculiar name later.)

Inside this book you will find a pair of cards, each with a unique code – one for you and another for the person you desire to become more compatible with. (A spouse, boy/girlfriend, children, friend, coworker, etc...) These codes will allow you to go online and complete your Flag Page assessments. [Note: If you purchased this book separately from the codes, you can purchase your codes online at FlagPage.com]

You will now be able to take our simple test that is designed to help you discover who you are at heart so that you can effectively and clearly communicate your needs to others.

This unique tool consists of three simple steps...

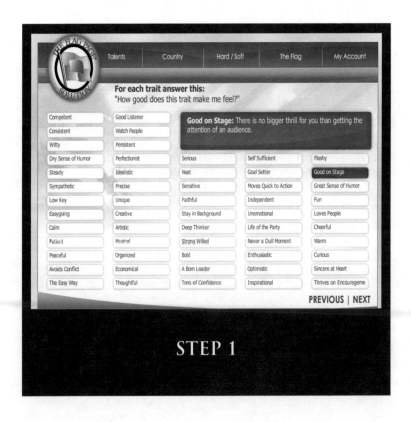

First, you are asked to choose as many traits as you honestly believe describe who you are. It is important that you do this from a general perspective, because most everyone CAN be any of these things. For example: Can I be "Low Key?" Sure I can. But does that generally describe who I am? Absolutely not! Therefore, I would not pick "Low Key." Just pick those traits where you can honestly and quickly say, "Yes, that is me." If you have to think about it for very long, you should probably just skip that trait.

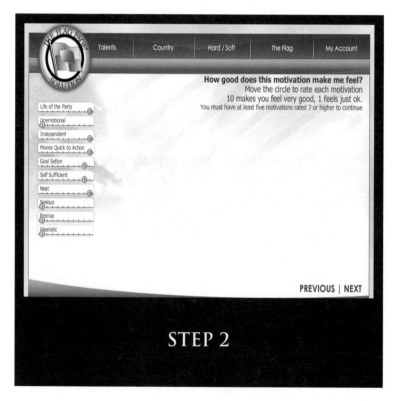

STEP 2

Now, on a scale of one to ten, you rate how good each of the traits you picked makes you feel. A ten means the trait makes you feel very good while a one means it just makes you feel "OK."

Choose one trait that feels the very best. Mark it by placing the "A" next to that trait. Rank the other four traits with the B, C, D and E in the order of how good they make you feel.

Life of the Party — A
Independent — D
Moves Quick to Action — B
Neat — C
Serious
Precise — E

PREVIOUS | NEXT

STEP 3

Finally, you decide on the five traits that make you feel the very best – in order of importance to you.

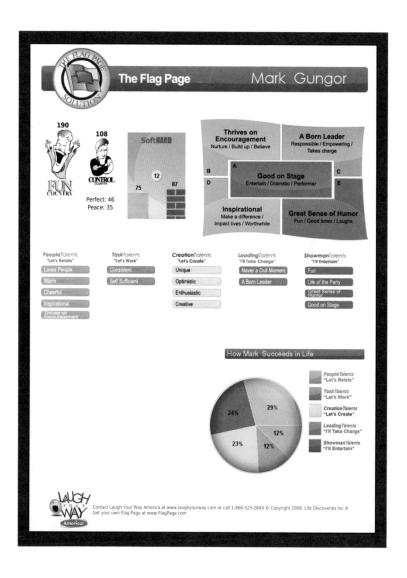

That's it!! In seconds, the program calculates your input and creates your custom FLAG PAGE.

A single, colorful print out that reveals:

1. Why you act the way you act.

2. Why you react the way to do.

3. What five things you need in your life to truly be happy.

4. Where you are most likely to succeed in life.

We will be using this printout to help you more clearly understand yourself and show you how you can effectively let others know just what it is you need from them. (Conversely, you can use this same program to better understand others.)

Chapter Three

THE FOUR COUNTRIES

CHAPTER THREE

THE FOUR COUNTRIES

When you were filling out your FLAG PAGE, you were unknowingly casting emotional votes for traits that belong to four distinct personality temperaments: CONTROL, FUN, PERFECT and PEACE. We refer to these four distinct and different temperaments as Countries. This is because the people from the four temperaments are just as different as people who come from four different countries. Countries have varying customs, traditions, ways of doing things, and certain words and phrases can have very different meanings.

Many years ago I was in Europe and had the opportunity to meet a young couple from England. They had a little boy who was a toddler and was just as

THE
FOUR
COUNTRIES

cute as he could be. It didn't take long before I found myself playing some ad lib game with him as he ran about full of life and giggles. At some point I said to him, "Come here, you little bugger..." Suddenly, his parents shot to their feet and in a fit of displeasure, grabbed their little boy by the hand and stormed out of the room. I was pretty taken back. I asked another person who was with us, "What did I say?" In his proper British accent, he replied, "Well, over here a 'bugger' is a homosexual."

I had meant no such insult! I tried to explain that where I come from the word had no such meaning, that it was not a derogatory word but, rather, a term of endearment. But it did not matter. As far as these people were concerned, I had called into question the sexual orientation of the apple of their eye, and they, despite my explanation, determined to remain offended.

That is what it is like when dealing with the four Countries. We love the language and traditions of our own emotional Country, and frequently misunderstand or become insulted by the others.

This stark difference is only exacerbated in marriage. Our differences attract us to each other. We sense that we could use the strengths that the other Country's resident displays. But then we get married and those very same differences drive us crazy. "If only you would be more like me!"

Marriage is not the only place where these differences show up. Parents from one emotional Country may not understand their child from another. The workplace often turns into an environment of tension when these Countries fight for turf. And church members of differing emotional Countries condemn one another as they fight for what their emotional Country considers proper and fair. We are even quick to quote the appropriate scriptures needed to validate our emotional Country: CONTROL people will refer to "being doers of the word," FUN people quote "rejoice in the Lord," PERFECT people prefer "be perfect, even as your father in heaven is perfect," and PEACE people are quick to point out that we should all get along and just "love one another."

In Florence Littauer's book, *Your Personality Tree*, she tells a story about her two grandsons who experienced the same event, but their "Countries" caused them to see the event in very different ways.

One night I called on the phone and Randy, Jr., said, "Have you heard the bad news? Ginger [their pet hamster] is dead. She died in her cage. I went to play with her and she was dead." He then delivered a fitting eulogy and gave me the details. In his [Perfect] way he told me how he and his father had found a little box in the garage, lined it with paper towels, wrapped poor Ginger in tissue paper, taken the box to a far corner of the back yard and buried her. "We had a funeral," he explained. "We'll always remember poor dead Ginger."

I was close to tears over his mournful musings of the memory of the hamster. When little Jonathan got on the phone, I said sadly, "I hear Ginger died."

He replied, "Yup, she's dead all right."

"Did you have a nice funeral for her?" I asked, giving

him an opportunity to share his version of the tragedy.

"No, we didn't have any funeral; we just dumped her in an old box with clowns on it, stuck her in a hole in the ground, threw some dirt over her, and that's the end of Ginger."

"Will you get a new one?" I asked.

"Well, we might get another one, but if that one dies too then it's bye-bye hamsters!"[1]

They both experienced the exact same event, but they saw that very same event in two completely different ways. Listening to one boy wanted to make you cry, while listening to the other wanted to make you laugh. If you didn't know it was the same hamster, you would swear it was two different events. That is the power of these differing Country temperaments. On your Flag Page you will see how you rated each of these "emotional" Countries, starting with the highest to the lowest. We refer to your highest score as your Home Country and the second highest as your Adopted Country. But all four have a say in who you are and help to explain why you act the way you do.

And before we go any further, it is imperative that you understand that the Flag Page is a reflection of who you are at your best and what you love the most about life. This isn't about what is wrong with you – this is what is right about you.

Let's take a look at these four emotional Countries...

CHAPTER FOUR

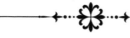

CONTROL COUNTRY

CHAPTER FOUR

CONTROL COUNTRY

Drive · Determination · Focus
Take Charge · Get It Done · Power · Serious

F irst, we have the rectangular shaped land of Control Country where everything in life is either black or white. Their number one cry: Get It Done! Their eyes can be steely and intense, their motions abrupt and they can put out some pretty strong vibes. Their voices can carry the sound of impatience and they are usually more interested in talking than listening. Their statements can come across as intense and their words can be quick, abrupt and to the point.

The shape of their land represents their hard

and very direct ways. The people of Control Country share the belief that it is absolutely necessary to control their own environment.

Their favorite vehicle is the bulldozer. They love to make a way where there is no way while they move on to higher and greater accomplishments. The down side? They can sometimes plow over the people closest to them, and they are often totally oblivious to the fact they are doing it until the people around them cry out from their flattened position,

"Hey, you're killing me!" The Control person may take notice, but will most likely respond, "Yeah, but look at what I've accomplished!"

Jonathan often found himself being untruthful with his wife, Jennifer. Not big, nasty lies, just little "omissions" and "creative reenactments" of the truth that was starting to really frustrate her. Jonathan was so focused on keeping the bulldozer moving that he viewed explaining exactly what happened as an obstacle, so he simply put things in a most "convenient" way or told Jennifer what he thought she wanted to hear. He wasn't motivated to be a liar; he just wanted to keep plowing.

After pointing this out to him on his Flag Page, it was easier for him to catch what he was doing. He learned that bulldozing the truth wasn't helping him. It was, in fact, slowing him down as Jennifer would confront him about his inaccuracies. He learned the best way to keep the bulldozer moving forward was to not create a situation that would require him to stop moving forward in order to fight with Jennifer.

Pastor Johnson was a successful church builder. In fact, he could go to parts of the country where no one had ever succeeded with a big church and soon would have a congregation of over 1,000 members. He had a unique sense for doing whatever it took to get results. Somehow, he always knew who could help him reach his goals. His record of success would attract talented people who wanted to work with him. These people would give 100 percent of their energies to help Pastor Johnson succeed.

Sadly, his staff members would soon notice that if they could help the pastor succeed, he would give them his time and attention. But if they had nothing specific to offer and just needed encouragement, Pastor Johnson had little to no time for them. As a result, the pastor found he had a continual problem of staff turn-over. His desire to "get it done" was so strong that others eventually felt "used" by him.

It is important for Control residents to remember that others are willing to allow them to ride their bulldozers to success – just don't run them over! The Control person's greatest desire in life is to be appreciated for his or her accomplishments. And while these people desire to be appreciated, it can be pretty hard to appreciate someone after they have just gone over you with ten tons of bone-crushing steel.

We see in the Control graphic that when they are not driving the bulldozer, these people are conducting the orchestra, always in the lead and usually running things – this is their favorite environment.

I should point out that these people are rather

unique. You see, most people from other emotional Countries consider the phrase "You're a control freak" to be an insult. But not these people. Being accused of being from Control Country is a badge of honor to these determined souls! Remember, this is a reflection of what they love. (By the way, if you accuse someone of being a control freak and they get angry at you, they are most likely not from Control Country.)

Look at the words Control people love to use and hear:

Grasp

Control

Get it done

Appreciate

Accomplish

Achieve

When you include these words in your message to them, they take great interest in what you're saying.

Control people's deepest need is to be appreciated

for what they do. Everyone likes being appreciated for what they do, right? Yes, but this need goes much deeper for the residents of Control Country. They don't just "like" being appreciated, they MUST be appreciated. If they don't get the appreciation they so desperately need, they will become depressed and despondent and will begin to seek alternate ways to find appreciation.

As we will see with all four of the Countries, it is this desperate search for what we truly desire that often gets us into trouble. A Control person may turn into a workaholic, since it is at work where he/she is most appreciated. A married Control person may find themselves drawn to an illicit sexual relationship because that other person "truly appreciates me."

Sadly, those closest to people from Control Country often fail to provide the appreciation they so desperately need. Why is that? Because everything about the Control person screams, "I don't need to be appreciated!" "I'm my own person!" "I don't need anyone!" "I'll get it done myself if I have to!" Now, they may or may not actually verbalize those sentiments, but it is what the people around them hear. Consequently, they don't give them the appreciation they desire. They think, "Why appreciate them, they appreciate themselves!" The wrong thing to do, however, is to deny these people what they need.

If you appreciate them, they become their very best:

Born leader

Tons of confidence

Goal setter

Independent

Moves quick to action

Bold

If they are denied the appreciation they need, they can become their worst:

Bossy

Impatient

Quick tempered

Demanding

Know it all

Arrogant

Control people don't always view the world like the residents of the other Countries. A Peace person and a Control person may both love people, but their underlying motivations can be very different. A Peace person may love people because he/she wants to make a difference in their lives. A Control person may love people because he/she needs them to reach their goals. The first may need people so he/she can inspire them while the second needs people so he/she can tell them what to do.

Oftentimes, Control and Peace people marry one another. Their differences attract them to each other as they can sense that the strengths the other person has are what they need. Sadly, however, after the wedding cake has been eaten, they get frustrated with each other because, "You're not like me!"

Control people can seem rather hard at times. But when you let them know you appreciate them and respect their accomplishments, the edge is softened. Clearly, life is better around a person from Control Country if the rest of us give them what they truly desire – appreciation.

REVIEW

Control Country residents are all about:	Getting it done
Their greatest need:	To be appreciated
Favorite vehicle:	Bulldozer
Favorite environment:	Conducting the orchestra, always in the lead and usually running things
Language:	Grasp, get it done, appreciate, accomplish, achieve
Their voice:	Impatient tone, talk but not listen, intense – quick words, abrupt and to the point
At their best:	Born leader, tons of confidence, goal setter, independent, bold, quick to action
At their worst:	Bossy, impatient, demanding, know it all, arrogant, quick tempered

Chapter Five

FUN
COUNTRY

FUN COUNTRY

Happy · Social · People · Mingle
Connect · Fun · Humor · Entertain

Next, we have my home: Fun Country. The star symbolizes Fun people's desire to perform and be the star of the show. Our battle cry is: Have fun! The jet plane is our symbol for high speed and no limits. Unfortunately, we have been known to smash into brick walls from time to time. Others around us may ask, "Why were you going so fast?" "Why didn't you slow down when you saw the wall coming?" "Why do you take such stupid risks?" But no matter what reasonable question is posed to us, the answer is always the same, "Because it was fun!"

Fun people love to smile. In fact, we smile when we are talking on the phone, even though we know the other person can't see us. We find humor in virtually everything, even when it may seem odd or inappropriate.

Several years ago, my grandfather on my mother's side passed away. Though I never really knew him, I thought it would be the respectful thing to do to accompany my mother back to Puerto Rico to attend the funeral.

During the wake, I sat back and watched

the many uncles and aunts I never really knew (Wisconsin is quite a long haul from the Caribbean) and saw that they laughed and seemed to find humor in almost anything – even at this sad occasion. Clearly, I come from a long line of Fun people.

After the service, the family carried the casket to the cemetery, and when they arrived at the grave site proceeded to lower my grandfather's box into the ground. As they tilted it downward in an attempt to put it into place, I noticed that they suddenly stopped. My Spanish is not very good (a result of being raised in Wisconsin), but I could tell by some of their comments that something was wrong.

Soon I learned of their predicament: The casket top had popped open and poor old gramps had slid halfway out. I was shocked and appalled by what was happening, but became even more shocked and appalled by the response from my mother and her siblings. They were struggling desperately to keep from bursting out laughing! In fact, the only one crying was a non-blood relative. I remember thinking to myself as I looked at these family faces, "No wonder I'm so nuts..."

Fun people can be very chatty and their big emotional highs are matched only by their big emotional lows. This, of course, can bring accusations that we are not very stable. We're stable alright; we're just always looking for fun.

Notice the words Fun people love to use and hear:

Really

Happy

Good time

Funny

Great

Fun

When a Fun person feels validated and understood, they become their very best:

Enthusiastic

Optimistic

Inspirational

Great sense of humor

Loves people

Sincere at heart

When feeling misunderstood and invalidated, Fun people can become their worst:

The people in Fun Country tend to constantly be on the go in search of a good time. This, of course, can irritate the residents of the other countries. "After all," they reason, "we understand about having fun, but can't you see there is a limit?"

The answer to that question is: No.

Besides, why on earth would you want to limit fun? Fun is what gives life its thrill and energy, right? Not to the residents of Control, Perfect and Peace. Control, Perfect and Peace people tend to view Fun people as an oddity. Their take on us is, "When we were children, we were like you too, but we grew up!"

Despite the encouragements of others (actually "wet blankets" from Fun people's perspective), Fun people are the eternal residents of Never-Never Land. To us, Peter Pan isn't just a nice story – it's a goal! Fun people have a strong need to be with other people because we don't like being alone. We put out a vibe that says, "Everyone is welcome," and enjoy visitors from the other three countries.

We want to be light hearted, likeable and we have a sense of humor about most things. All we ask is for you to give us approval for the way we act, and that you notice us – our strongest need in life.

While many people like to be noticed, being noticed is a deep emotional need for the residents of Fun Country. In fact, if we go unnoticed, we can become depressed and despondent and (in the worst case scenario) can start "looking for love in all the wrong places."

Here is the catch: Fun people desperately need to be noticed. The problem is everyone else thinks they've been noticed enough – so much so that they may actually go out of their way to deny them the attention they desire. They think that too much attention will "only encourage them," and, well... they're right. And that's the point; Fun people WANT to be encouraged by others. This can seem strange and odd to residents of the other Countries.

Fun people love to be noticed – even if it is for their blunders and mistakes. Many Fun people will openly share with others their most embarrassing moments or biggest, outrageous mistakes and failures. The residents of the other Countries sit in amazement that we can be so "open," "honest" or "self-deprecating." Actually, we are just wanting to be noticed. Notice us for our strengths, notice us for our weaknesses, notice us for our brilliance or notice us for our stupidity – we don't care, just notice us!!

While I was working on this book, I had to fly into Cleveland, Ohio, to do one of my Laugh Your Way to a Better Marriage seminars. As I was riding on the shuttle bus that took us to the car rentals, I could not help but overhear a woman as she was explaining to her husband why it took her nine hours to cross the small state of New Hampshire. She recalled in hilarious fashion how she and her girlfriend kept coming back to the same place – for nine hours! Then, because it was so late, they checked into a hotel for the night.

She told her husband how when they looked out their window they saw the biggest, fullest moon they had ever seen. What made it even more spectacular was that it did not seem to rise, but held its glorious position all night long. When they walked out of the room the next morning, they noticed that what they had been seeing was a big street lamp!

By now she had everyone within ear-shot laughing hysterically. It did not matter that a "normal" person would probably never admit to the stupidity of her trip. She was delighting her husband and the rest of us with her incredibly humiliating story and loving it the whole time. Why? She was a Fun woman who loved to be noticed.

Probably our greatest opposites are those from Perfect Country. (We can drive them crazy and they can really get on our nerves.) Perfect people love attention to detail – Fun people hate it (just look at my desk).

A Fun person can go to a mall, buy what they need, come back out and find that they have no idea where they parked the car. What's worse, they think it is hilarious. Residents of the other Countries (particularly Perfect) are mortified by such behavior.

"How could you forget where the car is?!"

"Why don't you pay attention?!!"

"What is the matter with you?!!!"

We, of course, think such responses are overly serious.

"Chill out!" would be our most likely response. Besides, there is no reason to have a cow. After all, it will be just fine. We then look forward to retelling the embarrassing story to the first group of people we can find. Why? Because it is, well...funny! Besides, we enjoy the fact that you are laughing with us and noticing who we are. Fun people's greatest dread is that they will be ignored and go unnoticed.

When I give my marriage seminar, I tell stories that people find hilarious. And they should – they are very funny. Like the time I was arrested and strip-searched for drugs. (Care to guess where they looked?) If the same event had happened to a resident from another Country, it would not be a funny story at all. In fact, it could be a traumatic event that potentially could have left the person scarred for life. Pretty wild, huh?

If it happens to me, it becomes a hilarious story that helps to underscore an important point that thousands of couples all across America have benefited from. Have the same thing happen to, say, a Perfect resident, and you have someone who may end up needing therapy.

Amazing.

REVIEW

Fun Country residents are all about:	Having fun
Their greatest need:	Approval for the way they act
Favorite vehicle:	Jet plane
Favorite environment:	Being around people
Language:	Really, happy, good time, funny, great
Their voice:	Smiles on the phone, humor in everything, chatty, lots of lows and highs
At their best:	Enthusiastic, optimistic, inspirational, great sense of humor, loves people, sincere
At their worst:	Talks too much, exaggerates, phony, irresponsible, undisciplined, distractible

CHAPTER SIX

PERFECT COUNTRY

CHAPTER SIX

PERFECT COUNTRY

Ideal · Exact · Precision
Feelings · Caring · Making a Difference

Next, we find the land of Perfect Country. These are the people that want to "Get it right!" If they were on the sinking *Titanic*, all they would be concerned about is that "The furniture has to stay arranged on deck!" – whereas we Fun people would be running around shouting "Woo hoo, we get to go swimming!!" unaware of our impending doom.

Perfect Country is the opposite of Fun Country. Oh, they can have fun – that is not the difference. The supreme difference with Fun Country is that while the residents of Fun Country don't like to pay

attention to detail, Perfect Country people thrive on detail. Perfect Country's diamond shaped land represents their longing for perfection with an inborn need to be precise and exact in all that they do.

If you approach them the "right" way they can be rather pleasant. Approach them the wrong way and look out!

Several years ago I was speaking in some one-horse town in Montana (small, to say the least). After speaking, we wanted to get something to eat, but it was like the entire town shut down after 8 p.m. Nothing was open! Finally, off in the distance, we saw an Arby's sign. (For those of you not familiar with American eateries, Arby's is a fast-food restaurant that serves roast beef sandwiches.) We headed towards the big, glowing Arby's sign.

When we pulled up, due to the way the store was lit, we weren't quite sure if they were open or closed. I got out of the car and pulled on the door. It was open! I walked up to the counter. There was a worker standing there with his back towards me, unaware of my entering the establishment.

"Excuse me, can I get something to eat?" I inquired.

Instantly, the employee twirled around and in his grumpiest voice declared, "I'm sorry sir, we're closed!!"

Then he paused for a moment and added, "... but the drive through is open."

I pointed at the drive-through window that was only a few feet from where we were standing. "You mean that window right there?"

"Yes sir!" barked the employee.

"Well, can't I just order right here??"

"I'm sorry sir, WE ARE CLOSED!!"

I turned around, got in the car, circled the

building and pulled up to the drive-through window. The employee leaned forward and gently said, "Welcome to Arby's. May I help you?"

WHAT!?!? A few seconds ago he almost threw me out the door. But now he is the model of professionalism and warmth. Clearly, he was from Perfect Country. As long as I followed protocol – got it right – he was very pleasant. But if I violated the published manual's instructions, then he couldn't function.

The demands of Perfect Country? GET IT RIGHT!

The train on the track is the vehicle of Perfect people because they want predictability and to know that they are going somewhere specific. If the rails are not exactly in the right place, the train cannot go forward. Perfect people are known for "stopping the train" if things aren't just right. As a result, they are frequently confused with Control people and often hear, "You are such a control freak!" They, however, do not desire control of their environment like the residents of Control Country.

In fact, when you accuse a Control resident of being in control, they usually smile and agree with you. When you accuse a Perfect resident of trying to be in control, they feel insulted. They are not trying to control things, rather, they desire that everything be just right before proceeding. In Perfect country, the residents can't stand it when things are wrong. They want to "get it right" under all circumstances. While Control people desire appreciation and Fun people want to be noticed, the residents of Perfect crave order and structure.

Because they so desire to get things right, they can use a lot of words to say very little. They worry if things are not just right and can remain serious and concerned as they hover over the details of life.

The illustration of the magnifying glass shows how these people love to focus in on detail. They can make details "come alive" and as a result, are some of the most brilliantly creative people in the world. This is the land where the great artists, writers, poets, musicians, inventors, architects and technicians come from. They are very creative and sensitive people and will warmly accept you if you use the words they long to hear, because you are then speaking their language:

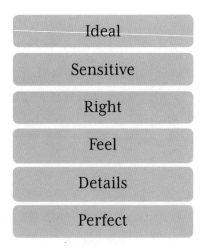

Of course, the magnifying glass also helps them to see what is wrong with, well...everything. That is most disconcerting to the residents of the other Countries. You see, for a Control, Fun or Peace person to tell you what's wrong with you, we often mean it as an insult. But one of the ways a Perfect person shows their love and concern is to point out what is wrong. They think, "I love you, therefore let me tell you what is wrong with you."

Of course, it does not feel like love to the residents of the other Countries and they do not always appreciate it. Sometimes, even fellow residents may not appreciate it! But they do not mean it as an insult or a slam. In fact, if Perfect people did not care, they most likely would ignore you. But if they care, they often show it by telling you what you're doing wrong, where you are failing, or in what way you can improve on what you are trying to do.

They have a great desire for order and can place it as a priority above all other things. These are the people whose office, work space or home is always neatly arranged. Some people with very high Perfect scores (we'll talk about the scores a little later in this book) are the kind of people who iron and fold their underwear, have their shoes neatly sorted, all of their socks are laid out by color and style, and if you pulled open any drawer in their house, you would see everything perfectly arranged and in order.

Their environment can be very important to them. For some, just sitting in an empty room with nothing on the walls or a messy, cluttered room will create a sense of stress and tension in them.

Perfect people are probably the most misunderstood people in the world. Those without this motivation cannot understand what the big deal is and may fight them in their desire for order. You can imagine how a spouse, children, friends, co-workers, etc...can easily mess with their need for order and neatness.

When a Perfect person feels validated and understood, they become their very best:

Sadly, they are often misunderstood, are left feeling invalidated and can become their worst:

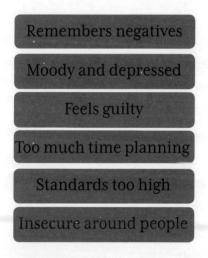

Perfect people can sometimes come across as tough and uncaring to others, due to their efforts to point out what is wrong and how things can become better. Others around them might assume, therefore, that Perfect people can be handled in a rough way. They assume, "Hey, these people are always throwing darts – I'll throw some right back at 'em, they can handle it!" But they can't.

The secret truth of Perfect Country people is that they are the most sensitive people in the world. Perfect people are always getting their feelings hurt by others. Because they feel things so deeply, they struggle to let these hurts go. Many spend years carrying around the slings and arrows thrown at them by others. Forgiveness can be a real struggle for them, not because they are hard-hearted – quite the contrary. They struggle because their hearts are so very open and sensitive to begin with.

What happens to a Perfect person who is wounded too deeply? They become damaged. Then they take the perfection that they long for and turn it on themselves, turning their desire for perfection into a deadly, self-inflicting weapon.

The breakdown of the family has been particularly damaging to the residents of Perfect Country. We estimate that nearly 50 percent of all residents of Perfect Country are in this painful category of what we call "Damaged Perfect." Parents who divorce, or who are abusive or dysfunctional in any way, inflict great damage on Perfect children.

In the same environment, Control kids just push their way past it, Fun kids try to dismiss it in as light a way as possible, and Peace kids make peace with their feelings. But Perfect kids take everything to heart, storing it all deeply in the vaults of their soul, hoping they can just keep everything locked away.

In his book, *The New Birth Order Book,* Dr. Kevin Leman refers to these "Damaged Perfect" people as "discouraged perfectionists" and describes how many of them are committing "slow suicide."
He writes:

Your perfectionism will cause anxiety and whether anxiety is conscious or unconscious it's got to come out somewhere. Certain parts of your body will pay the price. That's why so many [discouraged perfectionists] wind up going to see psychologists and the first symptoms they notice are migraines, stomach disorders, or backaches. They are the worriers of life, the ones who develop colitis, ulcers, facial tics, and cluster headaches.

Some perfectionists function very efficiently, but underneath the polished, seemingly flawless exterior is usually a person who wonders how long he or she can stay ahead of the posse, continually frustrated, perhaps wondering, "Why do I do these compulsive things over and over?" Whatever your degree of perfectionism, I know it is a burden and certainly a source of stress. And I also know from working with hundreds of perfectionists that the answer lies in controlling your perfectionism and turning it in an entirely new direction.[1]

Dr. Leman has written two books designed to help those who have become "Damaged Perfect": *When Your Best Is Not Good Enough* and *Women Who Try Too Hard: Breaking the Pleaser Habits*. I highly recommend these books to anyone who believes that their desire for Perfect has broken down, that the beautiful desire for creative and intuitive genius has been replaced by a self-destructive voice that tells them they are never good enough, that they can never measure up, and those who are constantly haunted with the feeling that they must constantly try harder and harder, no matter how successful they are.

REVIEW

Perfect Country residents are all about:	Getting it right
Their greatest need:	Sensitivity to their feelings
Favorite vehicle:	Train
Favorite environment:	Closely examining the details of life
Language:	Ideal, sensitive, right, feel, details
Their voice:	Talks a lot to say a little, worries if it's not right, enjoys lots of little details, serious and concerned
At their best:	Faithful, persistent, idealistic, creative, thoughtful, organized
At their worst:	Remembers negatives, moody, depressed, guilty, standards too high, insecure

CHAPTER SEVEN

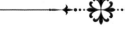

PEACE COUNTRY

PEACE COUNTRY

Harmony · Cooperation · Getting Along
No Conflict · No Disturbance · No Tension

F inally, we have the cloud shaped land of Peace Country – a land where you will find harmony and cooperation. Just as clouds move along at a leisurely pace, so do the residents of Peace Country. When war breaks out between the other Countries, Peace people quickly find a place to hide. When the bullets stop flying, they appear once again and quickly ally themselves with the winner. To these people, what truly matters is that we all get along.

The gondola is their vehicle of choice, floating gently on calm waters – swimming pools, if possible, since they don't like emotional waves. (Inevitably, these people wind up marrying someone who does belly flops in the pool!) Peace people believe that it is necessary for everyone to get along in order to obtain a stress-free lifestyle without conflict.

If you listen closely, you will hear the land of Peace in their voices – not a lot of lows or highs. They can be so laid back that they may not even acknowledge your comments. (This, of course, can really frustrate a Fun person, since their number one goal is that you acknowledge them.)

When a Peace person feels validated and understood, they become their very best:

Competent

Consistent

Witty

Patient

Peaceful

Good listener

When feeling misunderstood and invalidated, Peace people can become their worst:

Fearful and worried

Can't make decisions

Too shy

Little self-motivation

Resents being pushed

Resists change

Peace people are often very comfortable with long periods of silence during conversations. Why? Silence = Peace. The pauses can be very uncomfortable for the residents of the other Countries, but not to worry, these people just like to be in a state of calmness. Their calmness can seem to be a statement that they do not care or they don't reflect their deep seriousness, but just when you think they are being serious, they will surprise you with a burst of unexpected humor.

The illustration shows a resident of Peace country lying in a hammock while mowing the lawn. This is not laziness. It is a picture of efficiency to them because the people of Peace Country are all about low energy output while still getting work done.

They have very good social skills since they are so willing to be cooperative. But being cooperative is where they run into problems, because, you see, the residents of the other Countries are absolutely convinced that these people need what they have to offer. And since they are so "cooperative," they tend to be pushed about by one Country and then another.

Control residents say to them, "You know what you need? You need to be more productive!"

The compliant citizens of Peace Country politely agree.

Fun people come along, convinced that these people are in severe need of a caffeine fix, and offer to be their personal cheerleaders. "You need to be more excited about life! Come on! Let's go have a good time."

Again, the Peace people are quick to agree.

"Your problem is you're not doing things right!" shout the holders of the Perfect passport. "Let me show you how you can be better."

Of course, the Peace people quietly comply. After all, who doesn't want to do things better?

Indeed, Peace people are great to get along with and can be pushed about rather easily. Easily, that is, until you cross the one line that Peace people will not tolerate. That line is when you begin to insult them. For the Peace person's greatest cry is, "Respect me for who I am!"

If pushed too hard, Control people can make them feel stupid. Stretch them too far and Fun people can make them feel foolish. Admonish them too severely and Perfect people can make them feel worthless. It is crossing this line of personal insult, when you no longer respect who they are as individuals, that will cause Peace people to become upset and withdraw.

Kate found herself married to the man of her

dreams. He was a take-charge kind of guy [Control Country] and his bold and confident ways were what attracted her to Jim. It did not take long, however, for Jim to notice that Kate just wasn't getting enough done every day. As a resident of Control Country, Jim felt it was his sworn duty to assist his Peace wife in the ways of Control.

At first, Kate was more than willing to learn. (Peace residents are always willing to do whatever they can to maintain the peace.) But Jim started pushing too hard and soon he began to make Kate feel "stupid." Suddenly, Kate began to resist. She became upset and no longer was interested in what Jim had to offer. She would cry at the simplest suggestion from him. Life became difficult, romance was becoming a distant memory, and the harder Jim tried to fix Kate, the worse things became. Instead of "sufferable," life became "insufferable."

Jim's mistake was that he crossed the line you cannot cross with Peace people – you cannot disrespect who they are.

Peace people don't do well in conflict as you can see by the words in their language:

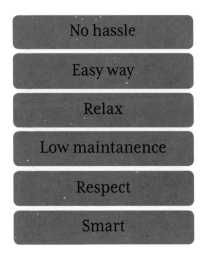

Their deepest need is to gain respect for who they are...no questions asked. They will allow you to give input into their lives, just as long as you are careful not to insult them.

The sad irony for Peace people is this: You cannot get close to someone without conflict. If you are from Peace Country, that is a statement I am sure you did not want to read. It is, however, the fact of life. Many Peace people run away from one conflict after another, doing all in their power to avoid confrontations. Sadly, in the end, they never achieve what they desire so desperately: Peace.

Those who deal with Peace people must constantly remind themselves that while conflict is inevitable and even necessary, insult is not. It's hard enough to get them engaged in needed debate, but if you get insulting – forget about it. The Peace person will completely disengage.

You can argue and debate with them. What you can never do is insult them.

Is it possible to argue and debate without insult? Of course it is. Just keep reminding yourself: Be nice.

REVIEW

Peace Country residents are all about:	Getting along
Their greatest need:	Respect for who they are
Favorite vehicle:	Gondola
Favorite environment:	Calm and productive
Language:	No hassle, easy way, relax, low maintenance, respect, smart
Their voice:	No acknowledgements to your comments, long silence is comfortable, no highs or lows in voice, very serious, surprise humor, concerned
At their best:	Competent, consistent, witty, patient, good listener
At their worst:	Fearful, worried, shy, unmotivated, indecisive, resists change, can't be pushed

CHAPTER EIGHT

THE IMPORTANCE OF UNDERSTANDING

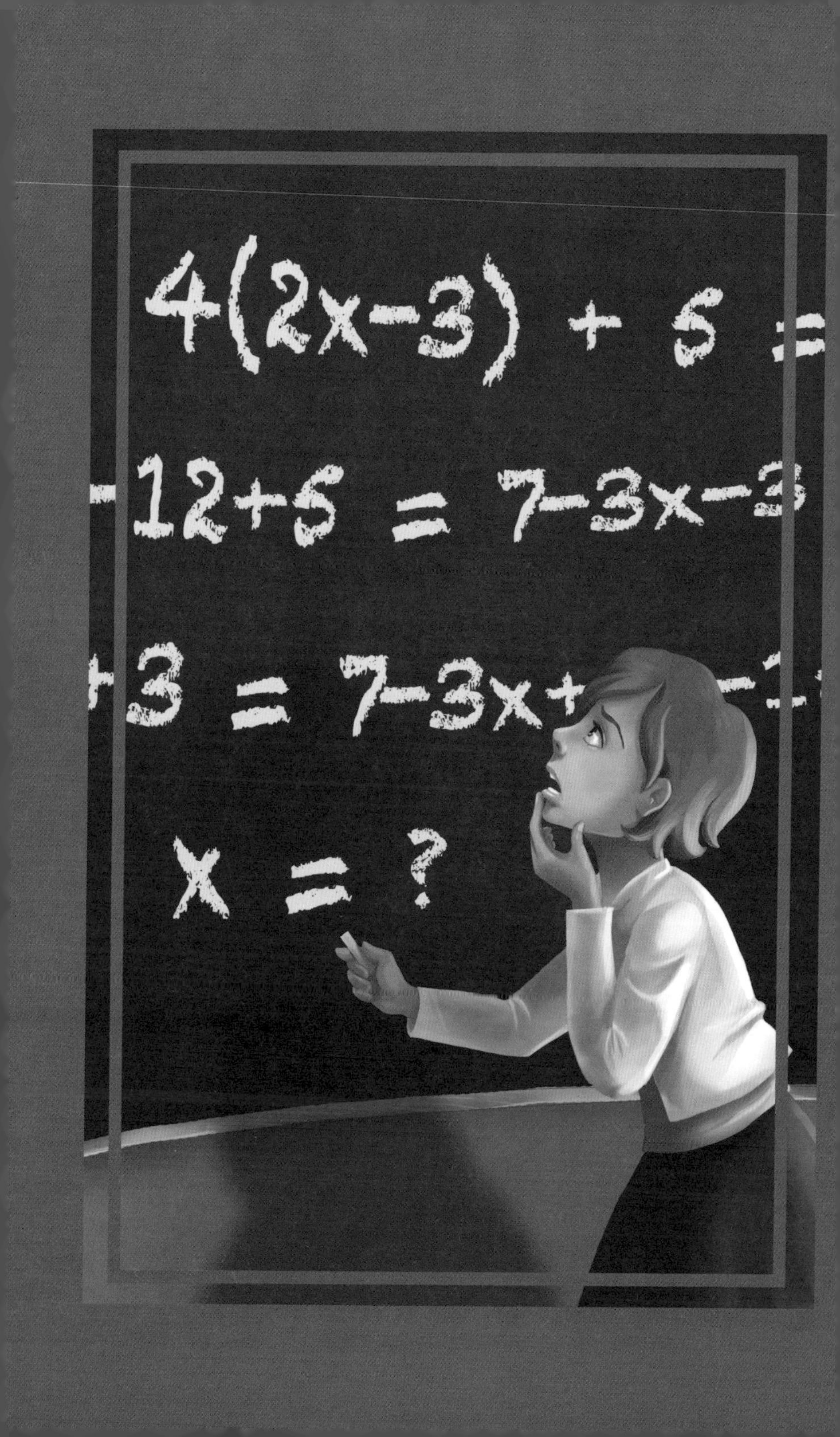
4(2x-3) + 5 =
12+5 = 7-3x-3
3 = 7-3x+
x = ?

THE IMPORTANCE OF UNDERSTANDING

T he importance of understanding these basic motivations cannot be understated. Without these insights, people tend to judge, criticize and condemn each other. Truth is, we all love our own Countries but feel there is something fundamentally flawed with the others.

When visiting another Country or attempting to influence one of its citizens, it is always best to speak in the native tongue of that land. This can be challenging, since everyone desires to speak the language of their own Country. The Flag Page is an effective tool in showing people how they can best relate to each other.

Here's an example: A Fun wife hears about my Laugh Your Way to a Better Marriage seminar. She is immediately hooked because of the title. She wants her Control husband to take her, so she says to him, "Let's go! It will be fun. We'll have a blast!" But she is talking the language of her Country; she might as well be speaking Swahili to her Control husband.

Better that she says something like, "I think we should go to that seminar. We will be able to learn some things that will result in better communication and allow us to achieve a higher level of success in our marriage."

Can you see the difference?

Keep in mind that, while it is important to do one's best to relate to the other Countries, it is equally important that people stay true to their own Countries and not try to be like someone from another Country. When they try to be a resident of a foreign Country, they'll seem like an alien who doesn't fit in!

A person who is not from Control Country, but tries to act like a Control resident, will most likely come across as being mean. Someone who is not a Fun Country resident will seem phony and irritating. Imposters of Peace Country will appear apathetic and disconnected, while those pretending to belong to Perfect Country will become frustrated and depressed.

Many married couples wish their spouse would become more like them. Truth is, however, you don't really want them to defect to your Country – they won't do it very well. Better they be who they are than try to be someone they are not. Besides, you were attracted to that other person's strengths for a reason: You need what they have to offer.

Finally, as we take a look at these four temperaments, keep this in mind: It is not likely that you will be described with 100 percent accuracy. Every person is an individual, and we do not assume that everyone in the world can be perfectly summed up into four categories. If God can make billions of people and no two have the same fingerprint, I think it is safe to assume that God has created people with infinite varieties of temperament traits.

I love the fact that the Flag Page takes this into consideration. While many other assessments simply categorize everyone into basic groups, the Flag Page shows how much you register in each group, as represented by the scores of each Country. We will discuss the scores later in this book in greater detail. For now, just realize that it is the combinations of all of these scores that show just who you are.

Having said that, there are a great deal of accurate generalizations that can be drawn from looking at your HOME and ADOPTED Countries.

Summary of the Four Countries

The highest score from your test determines your HOME COUNTRY. The second highest is referred to as your ADOPTED COUNTRY. These two combinations say a great deal about you.

We call Control/Fun or Fun/Control people The World's Greatest Leaders. This is because they have fun, but they still get things done, and people like to follow them.

Fun/Peace or Peace/Fun people are referred to as The World's Most Loveable People. And why not? These people love to have fun, and are able to easily get along with everyone. What's not to love?

Peace/Perfect or Perfect/Peace people (the largest group) are called The World's Greatest Workers. This is because they get along well with others, but are careful to get things right.

We call Control/Peace or Peace/Control people The World's Best Owners/Managers. This is because they get things done, but are careful of the feelings of others. This allows them to communicate well on a personal level while still keeping their "eye on the ball" of what needs to be accomplished.

Perfect/Control or Control/Perfect people (the smallest group) are considered The World's Strongest-Willed People. You better "get it done and get it done right!" These are the people in the world who would be the happiest if they owned their own island country and had themselves installed as the ruling (albeit, benevolent) dictator.

Our final combination is Fun/Perfect or Perfect/Fun. We call these people The World's Best Entertainers or Creative People. This is a unique combination in that it is a conflicted one. While all the other combinations flow easily with each other, this one is at war with itself. This is because Fun doesn't like Perfect and Perfect doesn't really care for Fun.

Those who have this combination are usually quick to confess that they feel this inward struggle, particularly if the scores of the two countries are very close. Those who don't understand these motivations within themselves often struggle as they swing from one Country to the other.

When they are having fun, they shoot Perfect in the head and can become slobs. When they are feeling Perfect, they can assassinate Fun and become mean and demanding. Those who have this combination need to learn that they can be both, and that they don't need to be at war with themselves.

CHAPTER NINE

UNDERSTANDING THE SCORES

CHAPTER NINE

UNDERSTANDING THE SCORES

As I said earlier, it is not likely that any one person will exactly fit any of the four Countries that were just described. The Flag Page system acknowledges that each person is a unique individual. It is when you look at the Flag Page as a whole that one is able to get the most clear and accurate picture.

The scores of the four Countries are significant because it shows just how intensely a person feels about each and every Country. For example: The higher the scores, the more intensely a person feels about who they are and the more likely they will display more energy than a person who has very low scores. An intense person will have very high scores,

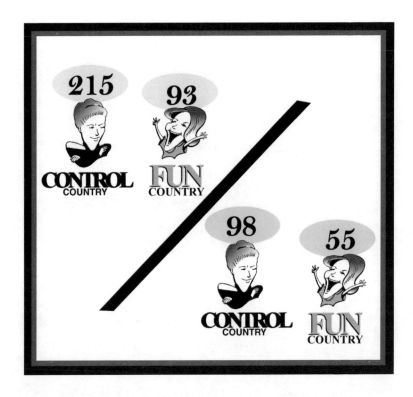

and a very laid-back person will most likely have very low scores.

Any score over 100 means a person is becoming very expressive in who they are. You can see that the person who voted for 215 will feel much more intense about Control than the one who voted only 98. Unlike many other personality assessments that place all Control people as the same or all Fun people as the same, the Flag Page allows you to see much more detail about who you are.

In the above graphic, you have two people whose results show that they are both Control/ Fun (Control being their Home Country with Fun as their Adopted Country). While they may share much in common, the first person who voted 215 for Control and 93 for Fun is very different from the second person who voted 98 for Control and 55 for Fun. The numbers help to reveal your unique, individual heart.

The person with 215 for Control will more likely be like the person we described in Chapter Four than the person who only scored 98. Also, the difference between the scores will show how comfortable a person will be in relating from one Country to another.

If a person votes 159 for their Home Country and 158 for their Adopted Country, that person can move much more quickly between the two than a person who would vote 159 for their Home Country and only 68 for their Adopted. The more "isolated" the Home Country's score, the more likely the person will be as we described.

What practical meaning does this have? Well, when a person has a much more isolated temperament, it is easier to understand and, perhaps, be able to anticipate how they will respond to a given situation. When an individual has scores that are very close, that person can move much more easily from one temperament to another and make it much more difficult for others to anticipate their feelings and responses.

This can make it a greater challenge to work with such an individual, or to have a son or daughter like this, or certainly to be married to this type of individual. Don't misunderstand, this does not mean these people are flawed, it just means they are different from those who are much easier to understand and predict.

What if a person scores very low in a particular Country? Well, if a person voted 0 for Perfect, you would have a person who would never make perfection a priority in their life. It doesn't mean they can't maintain order, it just means it is a very low priority for them. It also indicates how much understanding that person would have of someone from Perfect Country.

For instance, let's say a husband has a score of 159 in Control Country. Imagine if his wife scored only 16 for Control. That means she is not going to have much of an understanding of the values and beliefs associated with her husband's Country and may have difficulty getting along with her Control husband until she gains the understanding of what Control Country is all about.

In this example, we see a person who has a score of "0" for Peace. Does that mean the person can never be peaceful? Of course not. But it does mean that he or she is not likely to make "getting along" with people a high priority. A Peace person would start with the premise that, "We don't get people upset." Someone with a very low Peace score, however, may proceed with an attitude of, "Sometimes you have to get people upset. They'll get over it!"

Then there are those who score closely on all four Countries, making it possible for them to move from one to the other with a great deal of ease. These are the people who will find something to relate to in each of the previous chapters, but don't think any one Country clearly describes them. This is due to the fact that they have the unique ability to become any of the four that they choose at any time of their choosing.

My wife, Debbie, is just such a person. All of her four Country scores are very close, and while the Flag Page program will assign her a Home and Adopted Country, in reality she can move easily around all four. There is no one single Country chapter that accurately describes her. In fact, even though I deal with the Flag Page every day and have seen thousands of couples experience their Flags, even though I teach on these truths all over the world and even though I have written this book – I still can't "peg" her in one Country or the other. Why is that? Because she doesn't really belong to just one. She has that wonderful gift of taking on the traits of whatever Country is needed in any given situation. She can shift at will and I'm never quite sure where she will be.

On the other hand, the farther apart the scores, the less likely a person will be able to make the emotional move from one Country to another, thereby making them a bit easier to understand and, perhaps, easier to predict.

CHAPTER TEN

SOFT AND HARD MOTIVATIONS

SOFT AND HARD MOTIVATIONS

T here is no greater single chasm in life than that between those who desire to be soft, relational and flexible and those who desire hard, to-the-point results.

We even see it in the church. There are those who only seem to see grace, mercy, and understanding. Then there are those who are more concerned about truth, right, and upholding God's principles.

In his book, *The Grace and Truth Paradox,* author Randy Alcorn writes of the apparent struggle between grace and truth.

Truth-oriented Christians love studying Scripture and theology. But sometimes they're quick to judge and slow to forgive. They're strong on truth, weak on grace. Grace-

Soft	HARD
Calm	Competent
Patient	Consistent
Peaceful	Steady
Low Key	Persistent
Easy Going	Perfectionist
Sympathetic	Idealistic
Avoids Conflict	Precise
The Easy Way	Organized
Good Listener	Economical
Watch People	Serious
Thoughtful	Neat
Sensitive	Strong Willed
Faithful	Bold
Great Sense Of Humor	Born Leader
Fun	Tons Of Confidence
Loves People	Self Sufficient
Cheerful	Goal Setter
Warm	Moves Quick To Action
Curious	Independent
Sincere At Heart	Unemotional
Thrives On Encouragement	Life Of The Party
Witty	Never A Dull Moment
Dry Sense Of Humor	Flashy

oriented Christians love forgiveness and freedom. But sometimes they neglect Bible study and see moral standards as "legalism." They're strong on grace, weak on truth.

Countless mistakes in marriage, parenting, ministry, and other relationships are failures to balance grace and truth. Sometimes we neglect both. Often we choose one over the other.

Alcorn points out that Jesus was the perfect balance of grace and truth.

The apparent conflict that exists between grace and truth isn't because they're incompatible, but because we lack perspective to resolve their paradox. The two are interdependent. We should never approach truth except in a spirit of grace, or grace except in a spirit of truth. Jesus wasn't 50 percent grace, 50 percent truth, but 100 percent grace, 100 percent truth.[1]

Of the 56 motivational traits that people choose from when completing their Flag Page, some are considered very flexible and relational while others are considered very inflexible and results oriented. We call these traits SOFT MOTIVATIONS and HARD MOTIVATIONS. Notice that both sets of traits are good but just very different, and we tend to have varying degrees of both in each of us.

The Flag Page measures how a person feels about the Hard vs. Soft traits in their life. The scores over the Hard and Soft scales show how intensely a person feels about those traits. The scores show where a person is most comfortable. What is of greatest interest here is the difference between the two traits (the number highlighted in the yellow circle).

When the high score moves more than 15 points in favor of the Soft, that person is referred to as a SOFTHEARTED person. We call them Relationship People. They are generally more patient and flexible. Because of their relational nature, Softhearted people are interested in feelings, are good listeners and need to use many words to express themselves. Due to their flexibility, they also tend to see the world in shades of gray. Black and white approaches seem overly harsh and unmerciful to them.

When the two scores are more than 15 votes apart in favor of the Hard, that person is referred to as a HARD-NATURED person. We call these Results People – people who get things done. They are generally less patient and less flexible and see the world in black and white. To them, it is the truth that matters. Because of their results orientation, Hard-Natured people just want the bottom line and prefer to talk and listen in bullet points.

Hard-Natured people often get a bad rap in churches. Softhearted people seem so much more "spiritual" because they are so quick to apply mercy and grace. But Hard-Natured people are indeed wonderful and can be deeply spiritual. They know who they are, they are not as likely to be tossed "to and fro" by the winds and waves of uncertainty and can have a great deal of confidence about their faith.

If the apostle James called "double minded" people "unstable in all their ways," then he had to have really liked Hard-Natured people. They are not double minded about anything. They stay single focused on a task until it gets done. These are not the talkers of life, they are the "doers of the word" that James wrote about.

Softhearted people are quick to remind us that Jesus let people off the hook, that he said those who were without sin "should cast the first stone." True. But he was also the one who threw people out of church with a whip and the same one who called hypocrites a bunch of "snakes." As Randy Alcorn points out, Jesus was the perfect balance of grace and truth – what we call Soft and Hard. Bottom line? Both Soft and Hard people are valid and are important to building God's kingdom here on earth.

When a person's Hard and Soft scores are 15 votes or less apart, they are considered a Balancing Person. This doesn't mean that Soft and Hard people are "unbalanced." This simply means that these are the people who can more quickly and easily move between the Hard and Soft, tough and fair, grace and truth.

Balancing people can relate well to both Soft

and Hard people. They frequently find themselves becoming translators or arbitrators for the Hard and Soft people who don't understand each other. The challenge in dealing with Balancing people, however, is that they can change by the minute, choosing to be Soft and relational one moment and then suddenly becoming Hard and less flexible the next. While Soft and Hard people can be fairly predictable, Balancing people are much less so.

Again, take note of the scores – anything over 100 represents VERY strong feelings about these things. People with high scores tend to be very passionate and very intense. People with fairly low scores tend to be much less so.

The farther apart the numbers are between the two scores of Hard and Soft, the more difficult it will be for that person to move from one to the other. People with a high difference in the Hard and Soft scores (50 or higher) tend to have a very difficult time when they feel forced to the "other side" and will generally be very uncomfortable or even over-react.

For example, a person with a difference of 75 to the Soft side will feel very uncomfortable if they feel forced to the Hard side. They will often overdo it. These are the people who will "use a bomb to kill a fly." That is because they are so uncomfortable being hard and firm that they feel overwhelmed. They don't understand the world of Hard and often lack the appropriate skills that come naturally to Hard people.

The same can be true of someone with a high Hard score and low Soft score. They will become very uncomfortable and awkward as they stumble about trying to be relational.

SOFT wants to be emotional – HARD wants to be logical.

Hard people desperately want Soft people to be Hard, but when Soft people try to be Hard, they don't do it very well. In fact, they are usually terrible at it. They tend to overdo it and can become mean and very harsh. Think of the Incredible Hulk – "Don't make me angry, you won't like me when I'm angry." Bottom line, SOFT people make lousy HARD people. They don't become logical people; they turn into "The Hulk."

Then you have Soft people desperately wanting Hard people to become Soft. The good news is that Hard people can indeed become emotional. The bad news is that they usually do it with a negative emotion. They, too, become "Hulk-like" turning into somebody you'd really rather not deal with. Bottom line, you don't want to force a Hard person to become emotional. HARD people make lousy SOFT people.

Here's another movie analogy: Think of the original Star Trek series. Dr. McCoy represents the Soft and emotional; Mr. Spock represents the Hard and logical. McCoy and Spock always had a hard time getting along. Captain Kirk (think Balancing) would always step in between the two to make peace.

Whenever McCoy would try to be logical and Spock would feign emotion, it was always awkward and funny. Neither one ever truly understood the other. And all of us who watched, always enjoyed it more when Spock was just being Spock and McCoy was just being McCoy. The moral of the story? Encourage and support people as they want to be on their Flag – remember, this is who they are at their best. Trying to get a person to be someone other than who they truly are usually ends with very disappointing results. Let Spock be Spock and McCoy be McCoy. And the rest of you Balancing people can continue to play the hero.

Another truth to be aware of: Hard people tend to translate life in terms of right or wrong while Soft people tend to translate life in terms of friend or foe. This means that Hard people usually don't offend easily. If they don't agree with your input, they simply view it as incorrect and move on.

If a Soft person, however, does not like your input, he/she will not take your input at face value but will assume that you just don't like them. As a result, you can be very direct with Hard people (in fact, they prefer it) but you should be a bit more thoughtful when dealing with Soft people.

REVIEW

SOFT people are relational.

HARD people are results oriented.

SOFT people are more flexible.

HARD people are less flexible.

SOFT people see the world in many shades of gray.

HARD people see the world in black and white.

SOFT people need many words to express themselves.

HARD people speak in bullet points.

SOFT people tend to view input in terms of friend or foe.

HARD people tend to view input in terms of right or wrong.

Chapter Eleven

THE TALENTS

CHAPTER ELEVEN

THE TALENTS

At the bottom of your Flag you see your complete list of what we call TALENTS. These are broken down into five categories:

1. People Talents – "Let's Relate"

2. Task Talents – "Let's Work"

3. Creative Talents – "Let's Create"

4. Leading Talents – "I'll Lead"

5. Showman Talents – "I'll Entertain"

The traits that appear here are the ones that you rated at least a 9 or 10. These are the Talents that

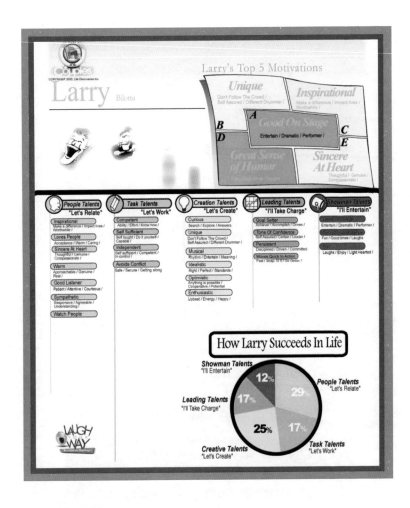

most influence and inspire you.

IMPORTANT: It is critically important to note that these are things that a person LOVES – not necessarily what they are able to do. For example: A person may choose a lot of LEADING TALENTS. However, he or she may not possess the skills necessary to succeed as a leader. The Flag Page just shows what you are inherently passionate about. It is up to the individual to obtain the knowledge and skills to succeed in any area.

Often, couples are interested in seeing how many traits they have that are the same. Some couples have a lot of matching traits (we consider five or more a lot) while others have none. What does this mean? Simply this: Couples who have a lot of matching traits will be different from those who don't have any matching traits – that's all. It doesn't really mean anything. A successful marriage is not about two people having a lot in common. It's about people who respect and support what the other loves and needs in his or her life – period.

Also, you may want to take notice of how many Talents appear in the Talents list. More than 25 is a lot. This may simply mean a person is very passionate about life or may represent a person who is struggling to become everything to everyone and can have a difficult time concentrating in just one area.

The pie chart allows you to instantly see where a person's core foundational interests lie by looking at your two largest talents...People, Task, Creative, Leading or Showman.

CHAPTER TWELVE

THE FLAG

THE
FLAG

F inally, we come to the part of the printout that gives the Flag Page its name – the five motivations that print out like a Flag. These are the top five motivations of your life, listed in order of importance to you.

This is like a picture of a person's heart.
What you see in your Flag represents who you are at heart and is the ultimate key to your personal happiness and satisfaction while interacting with others. If a person has these five desires supported in their life, it brings them joy and validation. If these five motivations are not supported, or worse, are criticized in their life, that person will struggle to

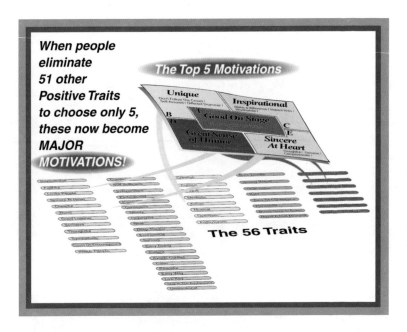

When people eliminate 51 other Positive Traits to choose only 5, these now become MAJOR MOTIVATIONS!

The Top 5 Motivations

Unique
Don't Follow The Crowd / Self Assured / Different Drummer /

Inspirational
Make a difference / Impact lives / Worthwhile /

Good On Stage

Great Sense of Humor

Sincere At Heart
Thoughtful / Genuine / Compassionate /

The 56 Traits

feel happy and fulfilled.

At the back of this book is an appendix that explains each of these words and phrases. It may be helpful for you to look up the meaning of the five motivations displayed in your Flag. And it can be particularly helpful to look up the motivations of your spouse, children, co-workers or any other person's Flag you are looking at.

But ultimately it is only your personal definition of each of these motivations that matter. Here is what I would suggest: Get your spouse (or anyone else you are trying to understand better) to fill out their Flag Page assessment (you can purchase additional codes at the www.flagpage.com site). Then get together and talk through each of the five motivations in your Flags.

Ask questions like:

"What does that motivation mean to you?"

"Why is it important to you?"

"Where do you think that comes from?"

"When did you first notice that in your life?"

Ask and answer every possible question that comes to mind as you both open up about who you really are. This simple interaction can be so powerful in helping people to understand themselves and each other. Through understanding, you ultimately discover what is truly important, and respecting these motivations will help you to truly succeed.

It is through this simple exercise of intentionality that you can begin to truly become compatible.

BECOMING COMPATIBLE

Epilogue

BECOMING COMPATIBLE

I like to warn single people that life is hard. And when I say hard, I mean really, really, really hard. That is why I encourage them to focus more on a potential spouse's character than on their looks. "Character will last you a lifetime," I admonish. "Sexy has a shelf life."

Remember, being compatible means being able to "suffer with." When people become incompatible it means their relationship becomes "insufferable" and they seek to end the relationship. What we all need are relationships with people so we can "suffer" through life together.

I don't know if you realize this, but the whole idea of "dating" is a relatively new concept – one that started to take root in Western culture about the mid-1800s. Before that people didn't actually date as we know it today. Truth is, for the bulk of human existence, most marriages were arranged.

As shocking as it may seem to us now, many people's first real encounter with their spouse did not occur until their wedding day. Yet consider this: Divorce was relatively rare. Why? Because people knew that couples did not fall in love, they grew in love. Or as I have laid out in this book, they became compatible.

As I stated in Chapter One, the key to compatibility is understanding. When you know why people do what they do, it changes everything. Oh, you still may not like what they do, but if you understand the underlying motivation it is easier to accept. If you do not understand the motivation behind the action, you will most likely become angry and bitter towards them.

It is also important to understand that just because a person's motivation moves them to act in a certain way, it does not mean that they have the right to always act that way.

For example: Let's say there is a woman who

is from Fun Country with a very high score. Since she loves to laugh and be noticed, she is disruptive in meetings or blurts out at inappropriate times in gatherings. To correct her by attacking who she is, saying something like, "You are never serious! You are always embarrassing me with your egotistical actions!!" would not be very effective. She would only view such an approach as an attack on who she is.

It is much more effective to adjust someone's behavior by first acknowledging who they are and then requesting a change in behavior. An approach like, "I know you love to have fun, and quite frankly, that is what everybody loves about you. But you are being a bit distracting by making smart comments right now," would more likely get the desired result.

Another example: A man who is a strong perfectionist is criticizing every move that the committee he is on is making, resulting in stifling the group and hurting creativity and fostering resentment. An ineffective approach would be, "You are such a nit-picking jerk, always criticizing everything people say! You are not always right you know!!"

A better approach would be to acknowledge and support who he is first and then asking for a change.

A more successful approach might be, "I know you are a really creative person and your desire to get things right really helps you shine. But right now you are frustrating everyone by constantly pointing out what is wrong. Why not let them speak first and then give your insights?"

You see, if you begin by attacking who a person is, they immediately shut down and don't hear what you are saying or asking. If you validate them first, making them feel safe, they will be much more likely to respond to your input.

What I have laid out in this book are wonderful tools that can help you clearly understand yourself and others. But you must be intentional about it. Learn as much as you can about yourself and your spouse. Try to understand the emotional Countries you and they come from. Discover how your Hard and Soft tendencies can affect the way you both react to things in life. And most importantly, take the time to talk through your five motivations – your Flags.

Be intentional. Compatibility doesn't come about by happenstance or magic – it happens on purpose. If you will follow the steps I have laid out for you in this book, you and your spouse (or kids or friends or coworkers) will learn how to truly understand each other and that will make it possible to succeed together. You will truly experience what it means to become compatible.

ABOUT

THE FLAG PAGE

T he creator of the Flag Page, Larry Bilotta, began developing the Flag in 1993. He closely examined personality tests such as the Myers Briggs Type Indicator, True Colors, DISC and several other tests, as well as the ancient Hippocrates personality rating of Sanguine, Choleric, Melancholy and Phlegmatic. He found the strength of these tests was in the depth and detail of how they accurately portrayed what a person would act like in life. But, these test results told more than was necessary. The questions to complete the test could run into the hundreds, and the multiple-page results were overwhelming. Due to the fact that these tests were created by psychologists and PhDs, the personality report summaries were complex and used words that only highly educated people seemed to grasp. Words such as "sensing", "intuitive", "dominant" and "analytical" are the language of the academic world.

In an attempt for a simpler approach, Larry picked a list of 56 character traits that described all four personalities while being careful to keep out any trait that seemed overly negative. He discovered that when people picked the traits they felt described them and then rated how strongly they felt about those traits, he could create an accurate printout of who that person was. Since their ratings were based on feeling and not thinking, it gave a clear picture of what drove and motivated people; revealing what they truly needed in their lives to be happy and successful.

The Flag Page is NOT about personality, but rather, about motive. Personality is too big a subject for most people to understand or remember or for that matter, even care about. Instead, people desire to discover their best motives in order to create a map to see how he or she can succeed in life. The Flag Page is that map.

56 FLAG PAGE
TRAITS AND SUPPORT TERMS
PERSONAL STATEMENTS

ARTISTIC
Doing more to make an attractive environment.

Good Taste:

I appreciate the finer things.
I know what is appropriate.
Be classy.

Stylish:

I know when it's good taste.
When it looks right, I know it.
Appearance does matter.

Skilled:

I'm competent at this.
There's a right way and a
wrong way.
I know what I'm doing.

AVOIDS CONFLICT
Staying out of tension and trouble.

Safe:

Let's keep things calm.
Everyone's feelings matter.
I do better without pressure.

Secure:

I need to trust you.
Can you reassure me?
I need your commitment.

Getting Along:

Let's live the golden rule.
We can work it out.
Let's accept our differences.

BOLD
Doing what's daring.

Determined:

I'll make this happen.
Persistence always wins.
Roadblocks are no problem.

Tough:

If you can't stand the heat,
get out of the kitchen.
You've got to be strong.
I can endure.

Takes a Stand: Together let's make it better.

Let's do the right thing.

Don't compromise the standard.

> ## BORN LEADER
> ### Taking charge and moving ahead.

Responsible: We have promises to keep.

Do what you said you would do.

I'll handle it.

Empowering: I'll back you all the way.

I know you can do this.

I can contribute.

Takes Charge: Here's how this needs to go.

I've got a plan.

Work together and get it done.

> ## CALM
> ### Creating the most stress-free life.

Quiet: Let's keep our wits about us.

Calm down and relax.

Let's take a moment and think.

Anchored: You can depend on me.

I'll always be there.

I don't waver on what's right.

Levelheaded: Let's keep an even keel.

Take it easy.

Stay calm, it's ok now.

COMPETENT
Being good at anything you begin.

Ability: I can do this.

I can do it, no problem.

There's always a way.

Effort: Let's give it some elbow grease.

I need to give it all I've got.

Let's go the extra mile.

Know-how: I know how to do this.

I see a way to do it.

I must get it done efficiently.

CONSISTENT
Making things stable and steady.

Stable:

Let's keep this the same.
If it's not broken, don't fix it.
Leave well enough alone.

Even:

We need to keep it going.
Keep it the way it was.
I need it to be predictable.

Predictable:

It needs to stay like this.
It's like this for a reason.
Leave well enough alone.

CREATIVE
Finding new ways to solve problems.

Anything
is possible:

There's another way.
There's an opportunity here.
There are no limits to what
I can do.

Innovative:

I've got a better way.
Look at it my way.
Let's try a new approach.

Inventive: Let's make a way to do it.
I can find another way.
It's in here somewhere.

CHEERFUL
Being pleasant under any circumstance.

Happy: I like who I am.
That's the way it ought to be.
Let's all just get along.

Pleasant: Let's all just enjoy ourselves.
Just enjoy the ride.
We can all play nice.

Friendly: Let's get together.
Let's accept each other.
We have things in common.

CURIOUS
Keep exploring, asking and searching.

Search: I need to look into this more.
There's got to be more to it.
I want to know the answer.

Explore:	I have to get out of here. I need to investigate this more. I'm looking for possibilities.
Answers:	Let's find a way. How does this REALLY work? Tell me what you really mean.

DEEP THINKER
Analyze everything in order to understand it.

Analyze:	I need to understand that. Where's the real meaning here? There's more to it than this.
Thoughtful:	I'm thinking of you. Here's something else to consider. I need to know why.
Introspective:	I'm going to find a way. Let me think about this. Look inward to solve problems.

DRY SENSE OF HUMOR
Coming up with unexpected humor

Witty:

There's a clever way to say that.
I see it as rather amusing.
I like the unexpected.

Unconventional:

There's another way.
Watch the crowd and
go the other way.
I take the unique approach.

Comic:

Let's look at the lighter side.
Life's too short not to laugh.
I see the humor in it.

EASY GOING
Allowing people to be themselves.

Calm:

You should chill out.
Let's just accept each other.
I'm relaxed and aware.

Go with the flow:

Let's take it easy.
Let's go with it.
Whatever...

There's always tomorrow.

Laid-back: Just chill out.
              Go with the flow.
              No reason to get upset yet.

> ## THE EASY WAY
> ### "Taking the path of least resistance."

Efficient: Let's not waste our energy.
              There's a better way to get there.
              Plan it, then do it.

Low key: Let's just stay calm.
              There's no reason to get upset.
              Don't rock the boat.

At your own pace: I'll get back to you on that.
                     Let's just take it easy.
                     I'm done when I'm done.

> ## ECONOMICAL
> ### Finding more ways to be financially secure.

Save money: I can get it for less.
               Now that's a deal.

I'll get just what I really want.

Careful: Let's be cautious about this.
Make sure it's justified.
Plan for everything.

Thrifty: Let's do the most efficient thing.
Here's another way to save.
I need to get the best value.

ENTHUSIASTIC
Showing people how I feel.

Upbeat: Let's make this positive.
I like "never a dull moment."
Let's take the high road.

Energy: I make things happen.
There's a lot more we can do.
Let's pick up the pace.

Happy: I like who I am.
That's the way it ought to be.
Let's all just get along.

FAITHFUL
Being loyal and true to a chosen few.

Loyal:

I'm here for you no matter what.
You can trust me.
Be true to yourself.

Committed:

I'm no quitter.
I'm secure with your commitment.
I'm dedicated to the cause.

Trust:

I'll be there for you.
Be there for me and I'll be there for you.
Please be dependable.

FLASHY
Standing out when going out.

Glamour:

I need to be a class act.
Everything needs the right look.
Fashion really does matter.

Stand Out:

Hey! Watch this!
You'll get a kick out of this.

Here's something you'll really like.

Show stopper: I think you're going to enjoy this.
Hey! Watch me now!
I'll knock your socks off.

> ## FUN
> **Looking for good times with everyone.**

Laughs: Let's all lighten up.
Let's forget your troubles.
Let's just have a good time.

Enjoy: I gotta love it!
Enjoy every moment.
Let's experience it together.

Light hearted: It's best if we all lighten up.
Why not forget our troubles.
Take it easy.

> ## GOAL SETTER
> **Staying focused on what I really want.**

Achiever: Let's do that now.

I can do more than this.
Let's take it to the next level.

Accomplish:

I made this!
I'll handle it from here.
I love being a winner.

Driven:

I'm determined to get this done.
I need to get a result.
Let's do something valuable.

GOOD LISTENER
Being willing to hear everyone's ideas.

Patient:

I can be flexible.
I can accept you as you are.
Let me learn about you so
I can help.

Attentive:

I'm all ears.
I noticed that.
I'm paying attention.

Courteous:

I want to consider your feelings.
Let me know how you're feeling.
I think of you first.

GOOD ON STAGE
Reaching the crowd by being up front.

Entertain:
Let me have your attention.
You're going to love this!
I love making music.

Dramatic:
I'll leave you spellbound.
I can make it spectacular.
This is going to move you.

Performer:
Ok, now watch this.
You're going to love this.
I want to teach you something.

GREAT SENSE OF HUMOR
Keeping my knack for creating laughs.

Fun:
Let's forget our troubles.
I love it when you accept me.
We can connect.

Good times:
Let your hair down for a change.
Don't take yourself too seriously.
Let's cut loose.

Laughs: Let's all lighten up.
            Let's forget our troubles.
            Let's just have a good time.

IDEALISTIC
Knowing it can always be better than this.

Right: That's the way it ought to be.
            I know when it's right.
            It's either right or it's wrong.

Perfect: We can make it exactly right.
            It can be better than this.
            Here's where we can improve it.

Standards: There's a right and wrong way.
            I won't compromise my values.
            Let's improve our ways.

INDEPENDENT
Standing on my own two feet.

Self-sufficient: I'll take care of this.
                   I'll rely on me.
                   I'm very capable.

Competent: Do it right the first time.
Just do your very best.
Show you care about your work.

In control: It's gotta go this way.
I know what's going on.
I've got the plan.

INSPIRATIONAL
Finding ways to make a real difference.

Make a difference: There's much more we can do.
Here's where we can make
an impact.
I see the need.

Impact lives: We're going to make it better.
I'm gonna shake your tree.
I'm thrilled to see you do better.

Worthwhile: Let's focus on what matters.
I need work to mean something.
Let's do something valuable.

LIFE OF THE PARTY
Making it happen so everybody has fun.

Exciting:

> Wait till you see this!
> Let's have fun and connect.
> It's intensely fun.

Happy-go-lucky:

> Let's forget your troubles
> and have fun.
> Relax and enjoy the ride.
> Nothing bothers me.

Center of attention:

> Hey! Watch this!
> You'll get a kick out of this.
> Here's something you'll
> really like.

LOW KEY
Keeping a low profile to not disturb anyone.

Stable:

> Let's keep this the same.
> If it's not broken, don't fix it.
> Leave well enough alone.

Secure:

> I need to trust you.
> Can you assure me?

I need your commitment.

Calm: You should chill out.
             Let's just accept each other.
             I'm relaxed and aware.

LOVES PEOPLE
Making sure everyone knows they are accepted.

Acceptance: I'm flexible.
             Let's be supportive.
             I'm grateful for what we've got.

Warm: Let's get connected.
             Let's find what's in common.
             Let's relate.

Caring: Are you OK?
             I want to know how you're doing.
             What can I do to help?

MOVES QUICK TO ACTION
Doing it now rather than waiting too long.

Fast: Why not do it now?
             Let's get to the point.

Is it done yet?

Snap to it: Let's make it happen.
                     No time like the present.
                     Let's get'er done!

Go-getter: This is going to be good.
                     Let's get started now.
                     Ambition is good.

MUSICAL
Expressing my deepest feeling through music.

Rhythm: I like a steady routine.
                     And the beat goes on.
                     Let's be consistent.

Entertain: Let me have your attention.
                     You're gonna love this!
                     I love making music.

Meaning: There's gotta be more.
                     I've got to make a difference.
                     I will impact your life.

NEVER A DULL MOMENT
Keeping a fast pace so it's never dull.

Hop to it:

I'll get right on that.
Why not do it now?
No time like the present.

Fast-paced:

Let's make something
happen now.
You'll need to keep up.
Get it moving.

Busy:

I'll get right on that.
There is always something to do.
The more we plan, the
more we'll do.

NEAT
Putting everything in its place.

Orderly:

Let's keep everything working.
Things are as they should be.
Keep it all in place.

Tidy:

We can clean this up.
Let's straighten some things out.

We need an orderly
environment.

Everything
in its place:

Let's make it productive.
It's better when it's neater.
Order makes things right.

OPTIMISTIC
Believing that most everything is possible.

Anything
is possible:

There's another way.
There's an opportunity here.
There's no limit to what I can do.

Cooperative:

Let's work together on this.
We should join forces.
Let's work as a team.

Potential:

There's more we can do.
It can always be better than this.
I have a vision for it.

ORGANIZED
Bringing structure and order to chaos.

Order:

All is as it should be.

With order we'll get things done.
Don't mess up my world.

Systems:
Let's go at this step by step.
I know exactly where it is.
Be more productive.

Structure:
Let's stay the course.
Let's do this right.
We need a system.

PEACEFUL
Giving people more ways to get along.

Calm:
You should just chill out.
Let's just accept each other.
I'm relaxed and aware.

Relaxed:
We should just take it easy.
Just chill out.
THIS is what it's all about.

Adaptable:
You need to roll with
the punches.
Let's work with what we've got.
I can go with it.

> **PERFECTIONIST**
> **Making it exactly right.**

Process:

Let's take it step-by-step.
Follow the system.
We should analyze this first.

Analyze:

I need to understand that.
What's the real meaning here?
There's more to it than this.

Ideal:

There must be a better way.
I think we should do more.
Here's something you
haven't considered.

> **PERSISTENT**
> **Never giving up no matter the obstacles.**

Disciplined:

I know what I've got to do.
Nothing takes me off my goal.
Where there's a will
there's a way.

Driven:

I'm determined to get this done.
I need to get a result.
Let's do something valuable

| Committed: | I'm no quitter.
I'm secure with your commitment.
I'm dedicated to the cause. |

PRECISE
Paying attention to the important details.

| Exact: | Here's something I've noticed.
I'll take a look at this.
I must have all the facts. |

| Details: | It's the little things that count.
It's all in the details.
Pay attention. |

| Accurate: | I can back that up.
I know this is true.
I know how to relate
and respond. |

PATIENT
Allowing people to be who they are around me

| Accepting: | I can go along with that.
Just live and let live. |

It is what it is.

Thoughtful:
I'm thinking of you.
Here's something else
to consider.
I need to know why.

Understanding:
I know how you feel.
I see the potential.
I'm sympathetic to
your problem.

SELF SUFFICIENT
Doing it my own way on my own terms.

Self-taught:
Look what I found.
Here's what I know now.
I learn it then do it.

Do-it-yourself:
I'll handle this.
Easier to do it than to explain it.
If I want it done right, I'll do it.

Capable:
I can do this.
I've got a good handle on it.

I'll take it from here.

> **SENSITIVE**
> Feeling what everyone feels.

Diligent:

I just won't give up.
Stick with the plan.
We need to stay steady now.

Thoughtful:

I'm thinking of you.
Here's something else
to consider.
I need to know why.

Considerate:

How do you feel?
How can I help?
All sides should be considered.

> **SINCERE AT HEART**
> Making sure that I and others are
> genuine and fair.

Thoughtful:

I'm thinking of you.
Here's something else
to consider.
I need to know why.

Genuine:

It's gotta be real.
Just be yourself.
I accept who you are.

Compassionate:

I make life easier.
I accept you are you.
I know where you're
coming from.

SERIOUS
Understanding what really does matter.

Standards:

There's a right and wrong way.
I won't compromise my values.
Let's improve our ways.

Focused:

Keep your eye on the ball.
I will not be distracted.
We must stay on task.

Important:

I think this could be significant.
Let's focus on what matters.
We need a purpose.

STAY IN THE BACKGROUND
Making sure that all is well and safe.

Supportive:

Is there something I can do?
Where can I help?
Just tell me what you need.

Encouraging:

Let me help you with that.
I see your potential.
I really believe in you.

Give credit
to others:

I admire what you've done.
I can see your talent.
You've got a knack for this.

STEADY
Being the one who is solid as a rock.

Predictable:

It needs to stay like this.
It's like this for a reason.
Leave well enough alone.

Productive:

There's something else we
should do.
Let's keep it moving.
We'll get it done.

Stable: Let's keep this the same.
If it's not broken, don't fix it.
Leave well enough alone.

STRONG WILLED
Making sure my opinions are known
and respected.

Determined: I'll make this happen.
Persistence always wins.
Roadblocks are no problem.

Leadership: I see your true potential.
There's more to you than
you think.
Are you with me or not?

Focused: Keep your eye on the ball.
I will not be distracted.
We must stay on task.

SYMPATHETIC
Showing people how much I understand.

Responsive: Let me know what you need.
Share so we can all learn.

I can take care of that.

Agreeable: I can see your point of view.
I know how you feel.
I'll do what you like most.

Understanding: I know how you feel.
I see the potential.
I'm sympathetic to your problem.

THOUGHTFUL
Thinking about the needs of other people.

Considerate: How do you feel?
How can I help?
All sides should be considered.

Caring: Are you OK?
I want to know how you're doing.
What can I do to help?

Warm: Let's get connected.
Let's find what's in common.
Let's relate.

THRIVES ON ENCOURAGEMENT
Finding people who will believe in me.

Nurture:

How did I do?
I thrive with your support.
Let me help you with that.

Build up:

Keep good feedback coming.
I love it that you noticed.
Thanks for being in my corner.

Believe:

Tell me what's good about me.
Consider my good points.
Make me a priority.

TONS OF CONFIDENCE
Showing that I am certain and why I am.

Self-assured:

I know I can do this.
I'll handle this now.
I know who I am.

Certain:

I know what I'm talking about.
I'm sure of this.
This is going to work out.

Leader: There's more to you than this.

I see your true potential.

I know you can.

UNEMOTIONAL
Being the one who is unshaken and steady.

Unshaken: I'd rather not react.

Maybe, maybe not.

That remains to be seen.

Steady: Let's keep it the way it is.

We'll just see.

Don't wreck my routine.

UNIQUE
Seeing and doing things like no one else ever will.

Don't follow   They just don't understand.

the crowd: I'm happy I'm different.

I've got the better idea.

Self-assured: I know I can do this.

I'll handle this now.

I know who I am.

Different drummer: I see it differently.
Let's try it a different way.
The crowd doesn't get it.

WARM
Finding ways to understand and
connect with more people.

Approachable: I'm always open to ideas.
Talk with me, I'm safe.
I see your point of view.

Genuine: It's got to be real.
Just be yourself.
I accept who you are.

Real: I need a connection.
Just be honest with me.
Please be genuine.

WATCH PEOPLE
Always staying the keen observer of life.

Observant: I comprehend it.
I noticed that.
Have you seen this yet?

Insightful: I have a sixth sense about
these things.
I know that I know.
I see the real story.

Curious: I wonder if there's more
to the story.
There's more to it than this.
What else could we do?

WITTY
Finding new ways to be clever and original

Smart: I know what it's about.
I get it.
I know this.

Practical: Let's look at this realistically.
Let's get to the point.
Why not look at the facts?

Clever: There's a smarter way to look
at this.
I think about it differently.
They never saw it coming.